CONTENTS

QUOTES

"Debra Miller did a fabulous job on this book! She blew me away with all the information she included on this topic. This is a must read for anyone wanting to learn more about their dismal future."
— *Stephanie Miller, Radio Host The Stephanie Miller Show*

"Depressing and yet surprisingly uplifting, but don't give up your Prozac prescription."
— *Sarah Silverman, Author, Comedienne*

"Not enough sex and no scandals! Jeesh! She gives away the plot on the first page! Still, there were a few useful bits, and she is paying me to say this."
— *Chelsea Handler Author, TV Comedy Star*

The quotes above are "creatively" written by the author.
If Stephanie, Sarah or Chelsea want to add their stamp of approval, she wouldn't say no.

INTRODUCTION

Ten years ago I inherited my father (hereafter referred to as "Old Guy" i.e. "O.G.") What was I thinking?

I became inspired to write this little book after listening to an audio program on my smart phone. There was an application which had voice actors read a wide variety of printed articles. This was a great service, because most of us love to multi-task and reading seems to be the one area that gets knocked out of rotation. The app pulled articles from self-help, tech, political, science and gossip. It helped me with my personal goal to know a little about everything, or as I like to say, enough to make me dangerous.

One day, I was half listening to an article about what to do if you become unemployed; a guide to staying sane, being proactive and hopefully land a job. The writer had many great ideas, but since I was currently employed, I was not listening too closely. But then the reader said something that resonated: *write a 30-page e-book.*

I thought (to myself as many people like to add, but I find annoying, cuz who else are you thinking to?) I can do that!

So what we have here is a gussied up, corrected grammar, elimination of nonsensical sentences version of my blog. It is well known that repeating the same thing over and over again is the definition of insanity and a sure-fire way to lose friends. Writing a blog is liberating, but the sad truth is that unlike an e-book one has to work to find a following (insert sarcasm).

In addition to my insightful and witty comments, I have added expanded sections on helpful devices (which may or may not be outdated by the time you are reading this) for aging bodies and what I refer to as "workarounds"–ways I have problem-solved challenges of geezer-hood via creative thinking, research, trial and error.

I hope that you are intrigued enough to read further. All 3 of my blog readers were.

THE BACK STORY

For many years my father and I had been estranged. I had always been a "mama's girl" so when my parents divorced, I remained distant. It wasn't for not trying–I did. Let's be diplomatic, I had a difficult time with his new wife. I was glad my mother was taking care of herself and did not think my father should be unhappy. If he decided to remarry, fine with me. There were two reasons for my distance: the "delightful" personality of this woman and the inability of my father to be able to balance the needs of his adult daughters and his wife.

Many years had passed with limited contact between us but I would always make sure that I knew his contact information and that he had mine. I would write to him about my life, but rarely received a response, which did not surprise me. My father is not an expressive man. Although I did not like that fact about him, I accepted his limitations. I remained in contact, but did not go out of my way to see him. It is what it was.

When my father's wife had passed away (it may well have been that day) he reached out for help to dispose of her belongings. It appears that when you have nothing left you call (estranged) family.

Thus far I haven't really exposed who I am. If you make quick Google search you will still know nothing about whom I am (there are at least 4,786 people named "Debra Miller"). I believe it is not easy or simple to sum up who anyone is. To know someone, you must peek behind the veil.

A bit of the story:

I was a poor white child raised in a black family, er wait, that was Steve Martin in *The Jerk*.

OK, let's fast track the childhood history. No tragedy's occurred. No abuse. No extreme wealth or poverty. We were a standard four-person nuclear family. I was fortunate to have gone to good public schools. I was fortunate to be an above average student, who enjoyed the said schools. I took dance: tap, modern and ballet, for most of my childhood where I was a hardworking adequate dancer. I loved my sister, who was 6 years my junior, always including her in my adventures. I loved my mother, who introduced me into the world of fantasy and storytelling through theater.

Really there is nothing exceptional about me...except perhaps my inability to stop talking and interacting with all kinds people. While my teachers found it annoying, it has served me well as a human being. I highly recommend it as a personality trait.

Goofy Halloween costume? I sure hope so.

Cut to: the teenage years. I had the good fortune to be alive and "coming of age" at the same time as the United States. By this I mean the 1960's. Much has been written about this time, but I'd like to talk about it from my POV. Indulge me, will you?

I grew up in Palo Alto, California. This small city has made itself known in all kinds of ways that influence the direction of the world. I know this sounds like a rapper's boast, but some simple research will prove me right. At the time I grew up, change was profound in the whole San Francisco Bay area. From music and literature, to human rights and technology–it was all happening! Including "Happenings". I was part of it all–the good, bad and the ugly. I, along with my generation, had <u>seen</u> our President assassinated. Sure, heads of state had been murdered before but not in front of the whole world. Television was changing our lives. When we protested the war in Vietnam, we shouted, "the whole world is watching". We were not going to sit still for injustice, in any flavor.

It is this early influence that set up my life. I proceeded to become involved in all the new movements, including civil rights, anti-war, feminism, and gay/lesbian liberation. I jumped on all the bandwagons of the time forming a part what I would call one of my personal mission statements: try anything once.

"How did that work out for you?"

I guess the best you can say is that a.) I am still alive and b.) I am not in prison. And as you can see from the following selections from my high school year book, it shaped my twisted outlook and offbeat sense of humor.

Two things to know about the following high school (Cubberley High School) photos:

1. I was not in ANY of these clubs (including the faux clubs).

2. I am wearing my usual outfit of black turtleneck and rose colored glasses.

Parapsychology club

Science Fiction club

Folk Dancing club

Far East Cuisine club

and last but not least: Fingerpainting club

Let's talk about the Gay thing. Did I know I was gay when I was a child? Simple answer: no. I was a non-conforming child, but there were no great sexuality insights. Apparently, some adults around my life had an idea when I was a teen...but I didn't get the memo.

Performing Anti-war theater: The Bozo Collective (with Laurie Garrett, David Talbot, Cindy Talbot M.D. among others)

I came out to myself after meeting some gay activists at the University of California at Santa Cruz. Ahh, this explains everything you say to yourself. It was just at the beginning of the LGBT movement in 1972. It was not a painful realization. I had little or no angst. I don't know why. Perhaps I am not prone to deep thoughts; it was just another fact of life for me.

It was at this point where I formed my second personal mission statement: political and social change occurs one person at a time. My theory was that if a person met me, interacted with me and saw that I was just another human being (albeit one who is funny, smart and charming!) they would go away from our interaction knowing they met a gay person who was not the horned devil that they had imagined. I have always figured out a way to enter my status into a conversation, unless of course, it was not safe to do so. I have never had a bad experience being honest about who I am.

It took a few months for me to come out to my mother. She was not thrilled, but after a little time, she was the loving supportive mother she had been before my pronouncement. My father was concerned it was his fault. I assured him it had nothing to do with him. Why is it that people feel they are at fault when it comes to another persons sexuality or gender identity, but not their morals or values? This is the first of many rhetorical questions.

I dove right in (there is a joke in there somewhere.) I was already very involved in the anti-war movement/feminism/criminal justice system reform, so being a gay activist was a natural step. It was a heady time for those of us in the bubble and safety of a university; we wanted change and we wanted it NOW. Age and hindsight have allowed me to see how important it is for young people to be so strident. If you don't make demands at that age when you have almost nothing to lose, when will you? Thinking that I wanted to change the world, I decided to go to law school. Law school was great, challenging and...not for me. I graduated law school, passed the Bar exam but did not want to practice law.

I wanted to move to NYC and become an itinerant theater worker. No, that's not what I "wanted" but it is what I did. Living in NYC during the 1980's was exciting and there are so many stories, but that's for the next book. This section is meant to merely illustrate my trajectory.

Suffice it to say, I got heavily involved in my theater addiction. Performing here and there, and even, by the grace of some amazing coincidences, on the Broadway stage in a show by Bill Irwin called *Largely New York*. During this time, I supported myself with various jobs as a set builder and stage manager. I learned to do many skills that I had not been trained in, and that opened my world. Putting together a desk from IKEA was fun! So when I had to re-adapt adaptable devices for my father, I was up for the adventure.

After New York, I did many other things: store manager for a piercing company, performance artist, Fashion Week production, film art department, event production. Each of these jobs developed a variety of unique skills. This knowledge base has become invaluable for my current role as Caretaker in Chief.

Here we are in 2014, almost 10 years after inheriting my father. Ups and downs, warts and all, people in glass house....Help! Stop me! I'm caught in an expression loop!

I hope this helps someone. If not, it sure has helped me.

THE DAUGHTER TRACK AND FIELD

I have recently realized that all my life I have fit into various current categories: baby boomer, anti-war protestor, radical lesbian feminist, sex-positive dyke, artist and now I am in the words of *The New York Times* ...one of *The Daughter Track*.

For the last 10 years, I have been living with my father now aged 92. I remember the beginning as if it were yesterday. It was the last night of Los Angeles Outfest Film Festival. I was in the Orpheum Theater and for some reason I felt my phone ring. I peeked at it and saw a strange phone number. Later that night, I listened to the message that would redirect my life.

"Debbie. This is Dad. Ann (his 2nd wife) died and I wondered if you could come help me."

The rest, as they say, is my life. I went to Fresno (that was the first sacrifice), assessed the situation and figured out that it would be mutually beneficial for us to combine resources. In Los Angeles, of course. I was willing to change things in my life, but a move to Fresno was not one of them. Many people say very nice things about what I am doing. It is refreshing to be on the receiving end of praise. But really I did not feel like there was another choice (and of course as I say that I realize there is ALWAYS a choice.) It just seemed like the right thing to do. So that was the beginning.

And oh so much more.

WHEN YOU SING YOU BEGIN WITH DO-RE-ME

Let's go back to the middle of the beginning part of this story. There I was a free wheeling lesbian, living her unconventional life, darting around the world (ok, NYC and London some parts in between) working, loving, creating havoc and doing a little good works here and there. Now I had become a "stay-at-home mom". And I didn't even get the joy of a new love. I did, however, get a new home and some furnishings that weren't culled from a resale shop or the street. I set up our new home in what I like to call "The Resort." This apartment complex was expensive but had all the enticements one could want. I loved it. We settled into a new life. I found O.G. a few Tai Chi classes aka "old people waving arms" at a senior center, and we joined the LGBT Temple.

Let's take a moment out to ask: Why do crazy people feel the need to SHOUT their inner conversation as they walk down the street??!!

And we're back from that commercial break. Joining the temple was a stroke of genius on my part. I did it because I found out they were going on a trip to Israel and O.G. had never been. I thought at the time, tempus fugit—he was 82. We went with 25 people we did not know, but upon return, we had 25 new friends including two women who have been helpful to me and O.G. Many people are gracious with their compliments in regards to my taking on the job of caring for my father in this his final chapter, but there are very few who come through with actual help, and these two amazing munchkins (they are impossibly short) have done that for me, for several years now.

THEY SAY...IT'S A VIRTUE

Sadly I have no patience. "Am I repeating myself, repeating myself?"

It is clear that I was given the "does not suffer fools" stamp at birth. All my life I have had to fight it. And for the most part, I have been unsuccessful. I am generally (and not in any order) snarky, sarcastic, demeaning, and rude. I do know it and because I know it, I have had to learn how to apologize.

"Wouldn't it just be easier to stop this behavior?"

"Ya think?"

See. Even in my imaginary conversation I can't help myself. I am a bitter old queen–this is not an offensive statement, because in my mind, B.O.Q.'s are quick-witted and wickedly funny. Sure there is an edge of meanness. If you had been attacked all your life you would too. This is the gay version of "The Dozen's" (look that up if you have no idea what I just said.)

Back to the original thought (and that's another thing about me: I tend to take side trips off the main story road.) I have a particularly low threshold for my need to repeat my statements, instructions, and requests. I generally go from about a 2 to a 10 in nothin' flat. I know this is wrong. O.G. has no short-term memory. I will repeat myself, for my benefit. He has no short-term memory. And yet I want him to use what remains of his brain to try to rationally figure out things.

Why do I do that? Most people are incapable of rationally figuring out things—see political situation in the US circa, well the whole life of the country really, but especially since Reagan. So why would I think this sweet 90+ man, who was never a Rhodes scholar to begin with could do that now? Just let it go, I say to myself in an attempt to calm down. Take a deep breath. Maybe start meditating. So why do I fly off the handle? Personality flaw they call it in AA.

Indeed.

DRAWING THE LINE

When I was writing in my blog, I would change the title of my posts on a regular basis usually when I thought of a more interesting and witty one (or at least I thought it was). But I think this title *Assisted Loving* would be perfect for my TV series, so streaming and broadcast networks, get ready.

The Lab Visit. For some reason the doctor (the last one in a line of fired ones—more on that soon) thinks O.G. should have some blood work. So I proceed to the Lab. One would think that would be easy a little waiting, a little poking, a little leaving.

But, NO. The Lab assigns take home duty (ah, yeah, that is a double entendre). Let me be clear. Fecal sample. O.G. is to follow a set of three steps of which I will not be a party to (yes, it is now correct grammar to end a sentence with a preposition). The directions were as difficult to understand as the activity they were requesting. It didn't go according to plan. And it was never gonna happen. I am ok with that. I ask what could such a test detect anyway? He has made it to the amazing age of 92 with his eyesight, walking only with the help of a cane. Sure he can't hear and his mind is going, but basically he is in ok shape.

I want to get serious for a moment (don't worry the hilarity will resume shortly). It is complex and trying to make health decisions for oneself, and doubly so for another adult. Have the talk with your parent about health, DNR instructions, and dying plans before it becomes necessary. And unless I am more powerful than I think, talking about sickness and dying will not make it happen.

This is my current philosophy on the matter of making health decisions for another:

The primary goal is to keep O.G. out of pain or discomfort. I will do what is necessary to make sure the pain is relieved. But if the answer is a major surgery or invasive tests that would indicate added medical care might be necessary, I weigh the factors. Will he die of the disease (or the cure)? Will his quality of life, as well as mine, be affected by the test or operation? The above description of the lab visit speaks to this point. If the test indicates he has colon cancer, will it be worth engaging in the steps to treat it, or are the odds that he will die before the cancer gets him equal? If his shoulder is deteriorating would a $70K operation be the right direction? Maybe the answer is a simple: just add two ibuprofen to the medication mix (and a glass of wine for me).

In my humble opinion, I really don't think I have to push on this.

Yeah, I know, more double entendres...and this is what my life has become.

WHAT TO DO TOGETHER?

TV is our common space. I try to watch a show with him every night I am home. I know it sounds weird, because watching a TV program with another human being is not really an interaction. But that is the best I can do most nights, which is better than the nights when all I can do is walk through the room and ask him what Vanna White is wearing or who is winning the game?

Definition of awkward: One night, I was watching an early feed of *The L Word* with Dad. At about half way into the show I realized that I was incredibly uncomfortable; that watching THIS show together, one that had previously given me enjoyment, was not ok. So the next week when it came on, I said, "Dad please go in your room and watch *60 Minutes.*"

"Why?" he asked.

"Because I want to watch *The L Word.*"

Then he countered, "I like that show!"

Exasperated I replied, "I understand but I am <u>not</u> comfortable watching it with you."

And then sometimes, I just drag O.G. along. I have several filmmaker friends who are always looking for extras. Being an extra is normally not for the fainthearted. Not that is hard work, it's just really boring. The day is basically hurry up and wait. This happens to be perfect for trying to fill many hours with O.G. Once he "played" (I use that word loosely) a gay man at drag-queen led bingo night. Below he is getting made up for a big dinner scene at a restaurant with the mother of director Blayne Weaver, sitting next to the stars Mark Harmon and Tricia O'Kelly, in *Weather Girl*.

I imagine that after a period of time all relationships come down to this: peaceful co-existence. When all things are considered (yes, I do love NPR), I think that just might be alright.

Make up artist Keri Ann Luevano hard at
work!

TO TRAVEL OR NOT. THAT IS THE QUESTION.

I think it's time to seriously consider my sanity. I say this, dear reader (you should feel special since you are the only one) cuz if you are my friend, you will say something.

I made a decision to spend the Jewish New Year holiday with my father's sister's family in Dallas. I must confess that my previous visits have been great. I really enjoy my family (despite their affection for the "R" party) and all the non-relatives I encountered were always super polite and friendly, so I have nothing but good experiences in the Lone Star state. Still, I am who I am—a dyed in the wool liberal/flaming gay and therefore admit to a certain amount of prejudice. It doesn't help that I recently heard a news report about voter rolls being purged in the state.

The last several trips have been fairly straight forward, but this one was anything but. It seemed to me as if we were acting out the wrong part of the Torah. I know it sounds more like Passover, not New Year's, with my version of the modern plagues or an episode of *The Amazing Race*: delayed flight, smelly rental car, hotel power going out for a day, change of hotels, drop off at the wrong departure gate followed by an OJ-type run through the terminal, fierce cold and relentless rain. I felt certain that each event designed to challenge my ability to remain centered in the middle of chaos. Oh, and did I mention that O.G. was seemingly more deaf and forgetful? But, what the heck. I made it tattered but intact to the finish line.

We went to celebrate 5773 years of disorganized existence, with our mispocha. On this night some Jews will go to temple, and some will have large family dinners like the one we will be at tonight. So in spite of the rigors of traveling I am glad to have that familial connection. Best of all, O.G. was happy. Priceless.

O.G. and sister Lois

Other times traveling can be fun...for a minute!

BUT I DIGRESS

So I have been busy living life and waiting for another funny bon mot to be created by O.G. and myself. Now that I have you suspended in space, I don't really have one. It's just more of the same "lather, rinse, and repeat" or for those of you who don't follow my skewed brain functions, this is my endless loop: I say something to O.G., repeat it, say it again, then repeat again.

"I did tell you, you have heard this before...now why would I lie to you?" Then repeat, bang your head against the wall, and hope against hope that someone loves you—or at least is getting paid—when you do the same thing in your very near future.

I went traveling last week, alone this time even though not taking O.G. with me involves an equal amount of preparation as taking him. I had to get away. I repeat: THERE ARE LIVES AT STAKE!

It was a celebration my friend's life (she had a "brush") in Seattle. But isn't it funny, or in this case ironic, that I go to see and connect with many people from the past, and on the first night I lose my voice! For those of you who know me, well, I am assuming that is everyone, or why are you reading this—unless it's that person to whom I am sending checks, you know that I love to talk. I love to tell stories, make non-sequitur jokes (see above) pithy comments, snide remarks (see above). But apparently, it was not to be on this weekend. My voice was gone. Zip. Nothing. And yet I had a great time using my newly found listening skills.

That's it. Gotta run.

10

SIR, YOUR TRANSPORT AWAITS YOU

We are waiting to be assessed for ACCESS–a service that picks people up who cannot take public transportation on their own because of physical or mental infirmity. It is in the obscure Arts District (you knew we had one in downtown L.A. right?) off the 4th Street Bridge. As you enter the warehouse a line of elderly, physically challenged individuals with their caretakers awaits you. Hulls of former buses outlined with dotted yellow lines, green arrows pointing to different types, amid a maze that would confuse the best minds to say nothing about those aging or suffering from dementia.

We arrive at 11 a.m. O.G. is finally called at 12:15 p.m. Not too bad. We walk up to the line of small desks that are directly across from the waiting seats and the front door. (By the way, when a person walks in, there is no sign or information desk. I found myself telling people to have a seat and their name will be called.) After the preliminaries are written down–name, age, address. Pulse and photo are taken. Then O.G. is told to the follow green arrows painted on the floor to bus # 2, alone (without my help). He gets on that bus, (which I must remind you all, is not going anywhere. Just parked). He sits there for about one minute when his name is called again, along with five others of like physical capabilities. They all are instructed to follow the green line into another room, staffed by what looks like ex-cons, not that I have anything against that...made to sit down, sign another statement of their inability to use the bus system, then told to go back to bus #2.

Each of these steps involves v-e-r-y slow walking of a distance of 300 feet, minimum.

Why, I muse, isn't it just a given that anyone over seventy-five can receive ACCESS? And really, does a person who has two broken arms and a neck collar need to PROVE they need the service? Why doesn't the government downsize the operation thereby saving money and elder humiliation? Just what percentage, I ask rhetorically, would be "gaming" the system? I feel it would be worth the loss if 5% even 10% were scofflaw! Too logical? Yeah, I thought so.

Ten minutes later O.G. is called by another worker for evaluation.

"What health conditions do you have?"

Dad looks at me and then upon my encouragement makes a guess. This invasive questioning continues for a short period. He continues to be unable to answer the questions. Then the questioner takes his pulse. (One more time with feeling!)

"You will hear within twenty-one days that you will receive ACCESS. If not, call this number. Oh, one more thing—follow the red lines to have your photo taken."

I try hard not to blurt out that I don't think he has physically changed in the last 35 minutes. Then, as if pigs were actually flying on edges of East Los Angeles, we were done. 1:00 p.m.!

Dad: "Why did we do that?"

And you wonder why my new hobby is drinking?

Various modes of public

transportation inside warehouse.

11

VARIOUS SMALL BITS

1. Bingo Bootie

The senior day care hands out prizes to the bingo winners. These typically consist of travel size products, plastic games, pens from insurance companies, cameras that retail for $3.99. Like that. Usually I send them back to be returned to the prize drawer. But one day O.G. brought home a prize that would turn out to be useful. The kids loved the checkers game for at least an hour of fun on Thanksgiving.

2. So You Wanna Help?

The several agencies that help individuals with transportation each have their own set of rules. Each agency contracts with separate private companies to accomplish this mandate. And so if one agency only takes people in a designated zone, they can't pick up in another zone. In order to facilitate the O.G. to the four times a week Adult Day Care at One Generation, we have to use two transportation agencies. After a surprisingly short wait time, I have a standing order for both directions. What I love about this arrangement is that I don't have to drive and I don't have to ask for favors from others! Previously to this present arrangement, I was very lucky to have a good friend helping out, but truthfully, one can only ask so much from non-relatives.

If you are a friend of a caregiver and want to help, offer to assist with deciphering the bureaucracy of the various agencies. That is the real work that will last long after you grow weary of driving.

12

HELP ME CHUCK LORRE!

I saw a note in a blog encouraging random tagging in my posts, ostensibly to get more eyeballs to the page. So I thought whom better to list than the jefe (Spanish for boss) of TV comedy, Chuck Lorre.* I do not know him, or imagine that I ever will. We are in parallel worlds. Mr. Lorre is famous. I am not. Mr. Lorre makes people laugh. I mostly make people cry. He lives in L.A.; I live in L.A. and by that I mean, the L.A. Mr. Lorre lives in is Beverly Hills, and the L.A. I live in is on the TV show *COPS*. But we do share a heritage and a love of numbers (see his Vanity Card archives–see my unread blogs 1-56). Plus if I tag him in my post, then maybe someone will read them.

Recently I have not felt much humor in my situation. For those of you who can not be bothered reading *TDT/Assisted Living/Loving* or whatever I am calling it, I will summarize: Long time past her prime dyke inherits aging (82 at time, now 92) father "Old Guy" (hereafter referred to as: "O.G.") and hilarity ensues.

However, I have not been feeling the hilarity. It's a lot of work caring for others. And I don't mean in the "write a check to the charity" kind of care. Perhaps it's the reason I never had children or why men have wives; taking care of someone else is HARD. Still, it's best to find humor in some corner or insanity will ensue. So now I laugh at myself. How crazy to think I can get him to remember something he's seen 10 minutes ago? That is bend over chuckle worthy! I am just nuttier than those kids on "Friends" or "New Girl." And they are kooky, weird funny! Yup, that's me all over: 60-something, tattooed and still wearing high tops. Crazy!

Happy 2nd of the 3 New Year's. (This isn't the Jewish one when you eat apples with honey and then fast. No not the one that you eat whole fish and blow things up, but the one that you get fall down drunk and watch some 7000 pound crystal ball projectile vomit to the ground.) I like the idea of multiple chances to start the year over and over and over again!

Debra Miller Vanity Card #1

I am a shameless suck up and I long for the day Mr. Lorre will view this and take pity on me and give me a job in a writing room even though I have no experience & by the way, have no experience.

I will get coffee, however.

* Chuck Lorre could be replaced by a plea to: Jenji Kohan, Jill/Joey Soloway, Kenya Barris, Tina Fey, Pamela Adlon...you get my drift.

13

LESBIAN FAMILY VALUES

I am sick of people thinking that family values belong solely to these typical primary family units. I am here to tell you that it IS different for Lesbians (Dykes, Wimmen loving Womyn, female homosexuals etc). Some of us have chosen not to raise rug rats (not that there is anything wrong with that). There are as many reasons as there are stars in the sky, but suffice it to say, we, made a choice. The option of having a daughter (son...maybe) take care of you in your old age, as I am doing for O.G. is, well, none. What do we do when the proverbial C Word, MS, joint replacement, homelessness, and just shit hits the fan? We reach out to our the extended family of ex-lovers. This is very different from the hetero norm, or even the gay men's world.

I have many examples of this, including my own.

Recently, I needed a new shoulder (years of lesbian sex had taken its toll...take that as you will). I needed someone to take care of me–it's hard to do almost anything with your right arm in a sling–and of course, the O. G. Who did I call? Yes, right after *Ghost Busters*, my ex-gal pal (let's call her Lynn) from the New York 1980's period. Now, Lynn had just been a year out of chemo-therapy herself. I had sent her some helping funds when she was recovering, since I could not get away to help her (see above responsibility). She volunteered to come out (some might say coerced–potatoes/potatoes) to take care of us. Did you see the date? 1980's. But it wasn't even a question. It's what we do.

Right now an acquaintance is going through a gnarly operation. She is staying with her ex and her ex's current partner. Legions of friends visit her, and I imagine some are even ex-lovers. Do you ever see that in the hetero world? Nope.

So in conclusion, I'd like to say: suck on it right wing, cuz lesbians have true family values.

#11: Be nice to one another.

14

SNEAKY IS AS SNEAKY DOES

A little while ago, I noticed the O.G. was slowing down. I went to the handy interwebs and did a little research on the next generation of support for walking. The progression from standard cane to a quad cane has worked for a long while, and is still good for short walks but now it was time to go to the rolling walker with seat.

Quad cane

One night I assembled the walker after work, while O.G. was watching TV. I asked him to give it a try.

"I don't need that!", he hissed with astonishment and outrage.

And because I am a glutton for punishment, I responded and cited all the reasons he did, in fact, need the walker. Then after exhausting myself with my own mishegas, I set the walker in the corner and left the room. About 15 minutes later, he came to my room to ask how it operated.

Rollator
walker

You would think that I would have already learned that particular lesson. Apparently not! Many days when the temperature is a cool 75 degrees (I do know how ludicrous this sounds to those outside of SoCal), O.G. refuses to go in the hot tub.

I tell him, "It's 104 degrees IN the tub, and you have a big fury robe to warm you up after."

Falls on deaf ears (literally). So I go to my room, ply myself with drugs and alcohol, and lo and behold minutes later, he is walking down the hall in his swim shorts and towel ready to jump in. (See the pattern here?)

Moral to the story: Concede early and shut the f**k up!

ANOTHER PRIME EXAMPLE OF HOW TO USE SNEAKINESS TO MAKE A PROBLEM DISAPPEAR

O.G. has acid reflux. With diet and medication, it can be kept under control. This is a good thing for me too, since I do not have to wake up in the middle of the night to hold the bowl when he projectile vomits or make a trip to the emergency room when the pressure in his chest becomes too much.

Thus, I have become a bit of a dictator with the kind/amount of food and how late he can eat at night. For the most part I have it down: eat early, eat fresh health foods, don't recline after a meal, and rarely eat out. The only problem occurs with the lunches provided by the day care center that he attends four days a week. They provide a very creative menu–Jamaican jerk chicken, spaghetti bolognese, enchiladas. I am sure these are great meals for the staff but probably not so great for many of the clients, each with their own special handful of health issues. Our solution: I prepare a sandwich for him to eat instead. I do find it ironic that ostensibly the organization is very concerned about relieving the caretaker's burden yet here they have added another. Note to reader: send an interesting ethnic sandwich (in my case sardines) with your O.G. and watch him be the most popular fella in the locked adult facility! After all, what do old Jews know from chicken adobo? (I am exaggerating for effect here; the Center is multi-ethnic and does have a Passover meal on the menu.)

Back to that illusive point–Is it soup yet?

Currently, I was told that he was very upset when he was not served soup. The kind and smart staff knew it was made with tomatoes (a bad food for reflux and arthritis). But O.G. just thought they were leaving him out. It was suggested that I purchase single cans of soup to be stored at the center so that O.G. would have soup with the rest of the people. Problem solved with outside the soup can thinking. Done. Sometimes the smart answer is the simple answer. K.I.S.S.: Keep It Simple Stupid!

PHOTO MONTAGE

If you want to look smart and cultured, use a French word when an English word would do.

My friend Flaca (aka Michelle my editor) says that blogs need a lot of photos. I think it's because she thinks people won't read anymore and need the quick visual equivalent to bright shiny baubles. She's probably right. Still, I do love me a juicy, well-expressed sentence. Not that I am the purveyor of that type of writing.

Anyway, back to the photos. Below you will see what things I attempt to do to keep the O.G. healthy, clean and safe. Naturally, all this depends on one thing and one thing only: **that he will actually read the notes.** One can dream.

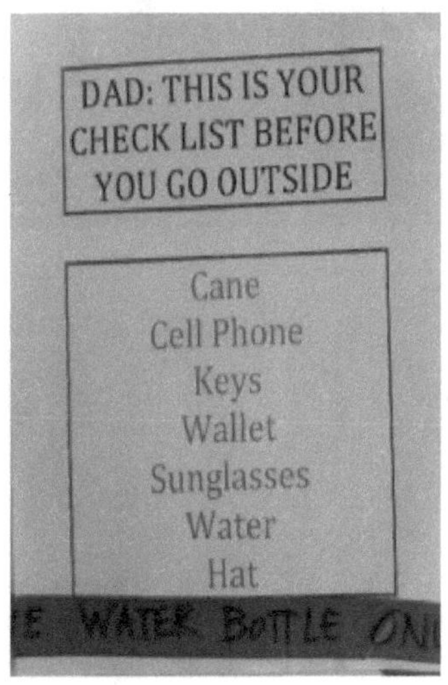

After a $90 Plumber visit.

YOU ONLY WISH IT WAS "GREY'S ANATOMY"*

So inevitably you will end up in the hospital. The usual way is via the ER. There are two ways to enter the ER: in an ambulance–where five buff paramedics tramp thru your house in the middle of the night–or by your own car. I have been through both. And by far, driving up to the hospital is better and for those of you on a budget, cheaper. It is better because you sometimes have the ability to plan your "visit". Here is a short list of what I bring to make it more comfortable: water, snacks such as cheese, fruit, nuts, crackers, charging cords, a tablet/iPad, electronic game, phone, sweater, comfy clothes, a split of champagne. And those are just for me!

Once past the front line (administrative desk of the ER), and through the maze of admitting, you are in the actual hospital room. I find it very useful to appear nice and knowledgeable even if only part of that is true (knowledge part). I make sure to learn everyone's name and let the staff know how much I appreciate their work. I put my phone number on whiteboard in the room and I call when I am not physically there. Getting someone to answer the phone, now that's the hard part.

One of the most important things you can do is to review the daily menu. Hospital food, while sucking in general, also sucks in specific. It's probably not true, but I feel as though the nutritionists employed in these type of institutions have not been made aware of the web or modern living, otherwise, they would be able to see that many foods on their meal plans are not good for the sick or elderly. I suspect that the diets were originally based on some formula written in the 1960's, and the current powers that be don't want to do the work of finessing the complexities of multiple diagnoses or probably more to the point, don't want to pay for it.

So I IMPLORE you to read, circle, make notes on foods that are inappropriate for, say, acid reflux, not just diabetes and heart disease, and bring in additional home made foods. It will make your Old Guy/Gal happier—never truly happy, cuz they would rather be home and frankly, who wouldn't?

- Keep notes if your memory is fading.
- Employ the friend network.
- Group texts help get the word out.

This type of support is vital to maintaining a positive disposition. But more importantly to remain out of prison for that homicide attempt.

*"Grey's Anatomy"–Am. Drama (nighttime soap) by Shonda Rhimes 2005-2021 (which I love & have a friend in the cast).

17

SO TELL ME AGAIN WHAT'S WRONG WITH BIG BROTHER TECHNOLOGY?

Like every good non-luddite city dweller, I have an iPhone. I love it. I have had several versions. Each gets better, and I know you can get a smart phone for less, but I readily admit I am a snob. I like Apple; I am from Palo Alto after all. So of course I have an app that tells me about other apps. And one day, I got a great lead.

This particular app was developed for people like me; we have upgraded to a higher version but could not give our previous phone away. So some smart developers figured out how to make the 2nd phone work as a remote camera. I like to call it "The Daddy Cam". For a mere eight bucks I can open my app at work, or anywhere, and see the O.G. sitting in his chair. This is important because recently he experienced blood clot in his leg that requires him to keep it elevated. With this new application, I am able to spy on him, and if he has his leg down. When he forgets I just give him a small shock on the collar... got ya!

"Dad, put your feet up!"

"They are."

"No they're not. I can see you through the TV."

Well, it makes me chuckle.

Sometimes when I check the camera, he is so still that it is often difficult to tell if he is even alive. But when the picture reloads, I can see small movements and realize all is good.

Here are a series of picture:

Note the leg in the down position:

After the call...

Alive?

YUP!

CARE AND FEEDING OF THE CARETAKER

IF YOU DON'T HAVE A SENSE OF HUMOR...NOW IS THE TIME TO TURN OFF YOUR COMPUTER OR DELETE THIS BOOK.

IF YOU DO HAVE A SENSE OF HUMOR, PROCEED ON.

And on those days when I am close to the edge, I show him this photo and say, "CAREFUL OLD MAN, OR YOU'LL BE PUSHING MORE THAN VEGETABLES IN THIS CART!"

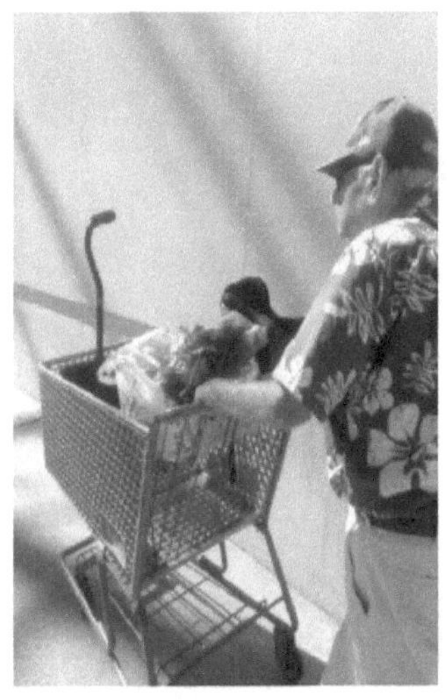

Relax people. It's just a joke! No need to call social services...yet.

I have learned that one must actually take care of oneself if one is trying to take care of another. Seems obvious doesn't it? This is not just lip service. It is mandatory to get away and leave all the worries behind. In the early days I was able to leave for a night or two by merely preparing food for those days. If I planned to leave for a week or more, I would take him to a friend's house. A few years later, I would have a friend stay at the apartment, as it was actually easier for him if he stayed in his own room. At this point (ten years in), I hire a caretaker. Although she is capable of real assisted care taking, O.G.

does not require that, so she basically is a cook and companion. It still is a lot of work for me to prepare to go away (shop, clean, laundry etc.) but I think it is worth it.

Oh, I know it's worth it, because both of us are still alive.

THE HANDY STUFF

So you have inherited the joys and sorrows of taking care of your aging parent. Of course, I don't know it all, but I do know enough. If you read my short chapters above, you may have laughed a little (hopefully), cried a little (possibly knowing that this too is your future) and learned a little from my so-called "journey."

Here is what I have learned: **GET 'EM EARLY**.

This may sound like the worst advice anyone could give to you.

You are thinking: Why me? This is not in my beautiful plan. I don't have time for this. I have to work/travel/take care of my children/domestic partner/wife/husband...fill in the blank.

The answer is: why not you? Statistically it is more likely than not for a child to take care of their parent at this point in time. Ok. I made that up. But basically it's the truth. Stuff happens. So there you are. The cold harsh realty has landed in your lap. The choices are to believe in whatever your rationale might be. It could be the 10 Commandments that command you to honor thy father and mother. Or fear could be the motivational factor: you could be cut out of the will. Or, maybe if you do this, you will get that cushy spot in heaven. Probably most of us just accept that it is a *fait accompli*. Belief or acceptance the result is the same. You have chosen to help your parent(s) through this last passage.

I encourage you to get 'em early because that is a good way to establish YOUR rules. And do not be fooled. Your rules will be the only thing that keeps you sane. Of course, you should NEVER tell them your plan. You should be sneaky and subtle just like they were when they were raising you. They should think that they thought of the idea. Equally important is for you to adapt to the changes that you will be making over time. It won't be such a stretch to go from leaving the ingredients for their dinner, to preparing their microwave meal. I like to think of this as evolutionary adaptation, not the big bang theory.

There are many seemingly little things that add up to a better quality of life for your parent and you. If your parent is relocated to your home, bringing them into that new environs when they are still compos mentis means that the neighborhood will become familiar to them. So when the dementia begins to take its toll, all the walking routes will be etched in the brain.

Or as Flaca likes to say: all muscle no memory.

One mistake I made was not establishing O.G. with the use of the bus. Most of us Californians, and I assume many other places, are in the habit of using our own vehicles. Since that will be a major factor in the life change and deciding when to stop driving, it might be good to encourage bus use as a way of prolonging self-reliance. Of course that could also be a double edge sword if Alzheimer disease is present. If you have transplanted your parent, like I did, it is important to get them involved in the new 'hood. There were several Senior Citizen centers within a five-mile radius which was important because at that time the O.G. was still able to drive there (through a series of right turns). One of the best things I did was to enroll him in Tai Chi. This helped with his balance and I believe, postponed the cane for at least 4 years. These Centers have many social events and educational opportunities. You will be glad they exist. Also if you live near a Mall, there are morning Mall-Walker groups, often with once a month get-together over bagels and coffee and a short informational talk by a doctor or lawyer. And when there wasn't a recession, they gave out SWAG.

My O.G. was not much of an active person for most of his life. A little swimming, a little walking–mostly to and from the car. He had several of the typical diseases: diabetes 2, high cholesterol, high blood pressure. And he was overweight. So in the beginning we discussed that he was to go on at least one walk a day. My mantra: Use it or lose it. To my chagrin (and fear of an elder abuse charge), O.G. likes to tell people with a grin, "Debra locks me out of the house." It's only partially true.

It has been my policy to start the changes early, before they are really needed. That way I can say, "I know you don't need it now, but I got a good deal on it. So I am just going to install this higher toilet seat or hand rail or hospital bed now."

I have made some timing mistakes. I noticed that O.G.'s hearing was going when I first inherited him. We went to the audiologist, but for some reason, decided not to get the hearing aids at that time. Then, as the loss became more profound, and all the adaptations I had made were not really doing the trick, I returned to the hearing professional. He was outfitted for a top of the line, high tech computer assisted, Bluetooth enabled, $6,000 hearing aids. What followed was two weeks of Laurel and Hardy type escapades. O.G. inserted the aids incorrectly or he would forget to put them in at all, while insisting that he did not need them. I attempted to return the hearing aids, but the audiologist pushed me to try again, which I did, knowing it was a futile and time wasting exercise for me. This might be where the "stand your ground" motto would be useful to adopt. Ultimately the aids went back.

SAFETY

Much like having a baby, you must make changes to the house. I was lucky that one of the bathrooms in our apartment was a shower only. Many people do not realize that the daily act of cleaning can be very dangerous, especially when an inflexible body has to step over a tub wall. But really the statistics show that it is beneficial to us all to consider these fixes.

"The most hazardous activities for all ages are bathing, showering and getting out of the tub or shower. (Only 2.2 percent of injuries occur while getting into the tub or shower, but 9.8 percent occur while getting out.) Injuries in or near the bathtub or shower account for more than two-thirds of emergency room visits." NY TIMES 8/15/2011 Nicholas Bakalar

This is very important both at home and on the road. When I was looking for a place to move into with O.G., I would only consider places that had a stall shower in at least one of the bathrooms. This is much harder than it should be, since, if I am right about this, we will all get old. To insure added safety to the stall, I did hours of online research, reading reviews (thank you faceless people who take time to write DETAILED reviews) and here are some of the options I chose. Support rails on flat shower door. These handles work ONLY on FLAT surfaces and glass is best. They are widely available.

This small product is great! It works on most surfaces, travels, and is inexpensive.

Mommy's
Helper Safer
Grip Traveler

I also spent some time adapting the toilet.

Elevated seat with cut outs.

Seat with footstool.

The seat screws directly to the sides of the toilet so fits both styles of toilets (elongated and round). I like that it has cutouts and is wider to sit on! I have purchased a small fold-up stool to help with, well, ya know, better evacuation, since the height of the additional seat changes the way the body sits on it.

Finding the correct medical team can be difficult for oneself, but for another it can be daunting. Since I had no referrals, I picked someone close. It seemed too good to be true–he was young, attentive and gay! We had a great time while Dad sat there, until... the day a condition that I had asked about and was told it was only indigestion, became an emergency surgery on a Friday night. First doctor: FIRED.

Then it was a series of tryouts. Finally, I found a doctor that spends time with O.G. in the room, is ON TIME and listens to me. As a caretaker, you are the one who best knows what's going on with the health of your parent. You are the one that sees the little changes such as noticing some blood on the clothes or sheets.

O.G. is so sweet and accommodating that when the doctor asks, "Boris, how are you feeling?"

He answers, "Fine!" (Perhaps you do that too?)

I believe that the word "patient" was made up by a doctor as a way to impart subliminal thinking. And, damn if most people don't adhere to their wish. I, on the other hand, believe I am a customer, and I want SERVICE. If I don't advocate for my healthcare needs who will?

I implore you, dear reader, be assertive. I utilize the following technique: talk quietly, express my feelings ("I am very upset/concerned/angry") but in a calm way. It's unnerving for them, but I get what I need. To close the deal and show them I am serious, I bring my Michelle Obama look-a-like friend with me.

Find your own way, but make sure you get your way. I also keep notes. I know when the test results have changed. This will impress the doctor and hopefully they will respect you. When you can respond in their language, it's like the tumblers in the lock have aligned and suddenly you become an intelligent ally and not a harping foe.

I realized that an emergency could happen at anytime and information saves lives. Knowing he could not or may not be able to communicate his health info, I started to look into the various options for a USB drive to wear on the wrist. I found quite a few options.

(Caveat MAY BE WAY OUT OF DATE 2020) In the end, I purchased a micro USB card (Amazon), wrote up all the health info (Meds, diseases/conditions, doctors, POA info, past hospital visits, etc.) saved it as a PDF, which is easy to open on any platform, and found a $13 Velcro wrist band (Amazon) to hide it in.

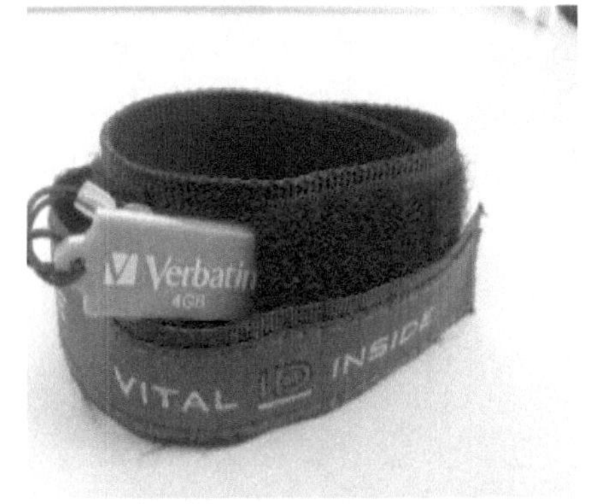

If your parent does not already have a mobile phone, and they do not need a big plan, I suggest going with the Jitterbug/Great Call . The handsets have large numbers and there are a few choices, including a handset that is stripped to the essence with large keypad. After having that version for a few years, I wanted to find something that would cover what I like to call "I've fallen/got lost/find me phone." When paying my phone bill online, I noticed that they had come up with a new service that incorporated all I wanted: a phone and a 24/7-response service that will tell him where he is if lost and then call me. He didn't have to learn a new skill, just open the phone and press 5* (star).

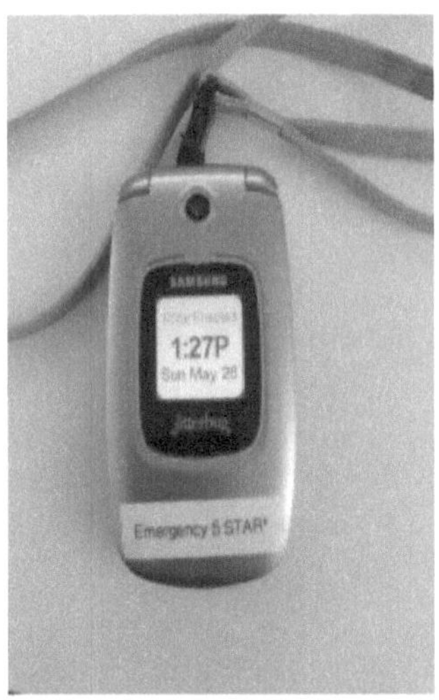

Low-cost phone/GPS/live help

Currently we have progressed to the next stage. Since he can't hear on the cell phone anymore, I have purchased a new device for emergency only, which is now hanging around O.G.'s neck. It has an smartphone app (GreatCall Link), which allows me to know when he is in a new location-at the Daycare Center or home, as well as any other locations I enter into the matrix. Sure, the personal liberties issues rage in the background, but I am happy to be able to track him.

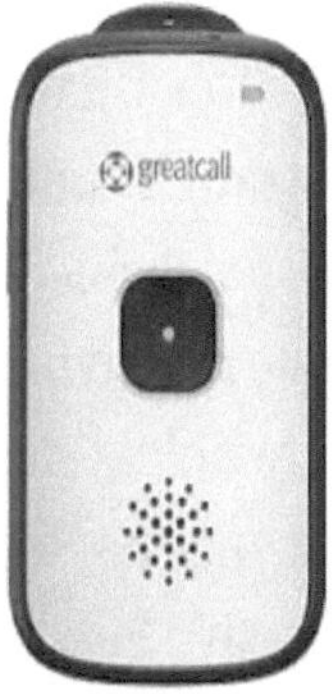

Emergency Help Only

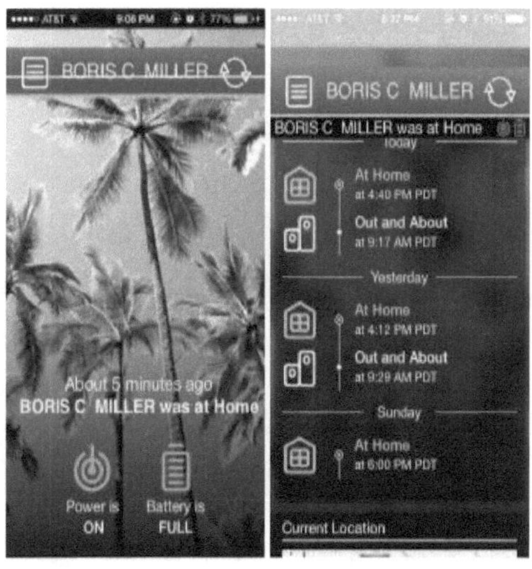

Other electronics will be helpful, just as they are for most of us these days. A computer or tablet will encourage communication with the world and family members. I also found that a handheld electronic game console has provided hours, ne years of fun. I purchased one type of game: Solitaire. Although there are 101 versions, O.G. likes one and one only: *Double Klondike.* The man knows what he likes in small portable electronic games!

When I missed the boat on hearing aids, I had to become creative about sound. First thing to remember is: do not try to answer a question from another room. Stop what you are doing and face your elder. It will save you frustration and ultimately save you from stroking out over it. Then you must find a way to enhance the volume of the television or radio without driving yourself or your neighbors crazy. I purchased a series of wireless headsets. Most of them were a waste of money (especially the one "As Seen on TV").

Ultimately, I took an inexpensive headset, purchased a 16' extension cord online and plugged it into the TV set in his room. This enables him to have the sound directly and again, saves two lives.

In the living room, where the main television set resides, I was unwilling to purchase the expensive surround sound system (possibly a mistake in hindsight). It seems that the new sets do not allow for a quick cheap fix by simply plugging in small speakers. I found one speaker meant for enhancing sound Original Dialogue Loudspeaker. It plugs in easily and when set up next to the good ear, works well. And don't forget to switch on the close caption function. It can be a bit annoying to the viewing of the picture, but will help with the understanding of the show greatly.

**(I am not receiving any money for this or any other plug... although again, I wouldn't object to it)

20

END OF LIFE DECISIONS: MAJICK!

UPDATE (JANUARY 2016)

The amazing thing about the digital book format is the ability to add a chapter AFTER the book is published and deliver it magically (ok not so magically for those that understand the programming languages) to all of you wonderful people who previously bought my little book. But I must tell you that this is not the chapter I had thought I would be writing.

Paraphrasing the words of one of the greatest evil politician in the U.S., Donald Rumsfeld–"you write the chapter you have, not the one you thought you might have." So without further ado (cuz I love my "ado's"):

This is THE chapter for everyone in the world!

I realize this is a bold(ed) statement but I assure you, I can back it up with facts and logic.

********News Flash********

(imagine these words below projected on a TIMES SQUARE-like marquee)

YOU WILL DIE.

You say you know, *but do you?*

Currently we are experiencing a resurgence of magical thinking. What do I mean by this? I will give you a small sampling of the concept of "magical thinking":

" You will lose weight; you will find the perfect lover; she will marry you; he will be faithful; you will lose weight; the world will come to its senses by ending war and hatred; the US will get universal health care."

See where I am going with this? It is the same for the subject of death. Many people think that if a person talks about the death of yourself or another person, it will hasten the event. I am here to tell you that is not true! I have done the scientific research. Trust me on this– the less said the better.

So given that undeniable fact, examining the eventuality of your death will not make it happen.

I am not a magician (although I did go to the Magic Castle once) but I am going to predict that 93% of you have done NOTHING in preparation.

- No final Will.
- No names on the bottom of your belongings.
- No filling out of the Beneficiaries line on your very small 401(k).
- And certainly no discussion of how you want to be disposed of with your loved ones.

I get it. It's annoying, it's painful and there is always something more interesting to do ("Squirrel!")

But if you care about those you love, you will at least consider taking care of these chores. Promise me that you will–at the very least–think about it. Or better yet, write your wishes down. The best thing would be to bite the bullet, do the minimum research and make some f*cking decisions.

I am enclosing links to a Will form you can write yourself. If you have more than a minimum of possessions–property, children/pets/old people or a more complex estate, you <u>must</u> see a lawyer for estate planning.

What happens when I croak? What are the decisions?

How will the/my body be dealt with? Will I be embalmed, buried within 3 days, cremated, or have heavy weights attached for late night time dumping? Will there be a religious ceremony, wake, or blowout party? Interested people–the ones stuck taking care of your gelatinous remains aka your hot (cold) mess–want to know!

Imagine if you will this scenario:

Your bestie calls. You don't respond...because you are d-e-a-d! In a day, if you're lucky–three if not–she gets worried. "Where is that beeyatch?" She decides to drive the 10 miles to check only to find you very bloated...and dead. What does she do? You never talked about it and now she must rummage through your stuff to find out if you were kind enough to write something down. The above questions are now running around in her mind.

Be a friend and DO NOT let this happen.

Legal Papers

Making a Simple Will – The State Bar of California

Make sure to search your state, since there may be some variations in the law. The best actions you can take are to assign any accounts that offer a "Beneficiary " option to the individual you want to receive it. It will go directly to that person (once the account is notified) without any other actions by the state, meaning NO PROBATE. Insurance, 401(k), even bank accounts have a "Payable on Death-POD" option.

If you have the more complex situations outlined above, you <u>should</u> contact a lawyer. If you do not know of one–and how is that possible?!–contact the State Bar of your state and they will guide you to some. Remember, this person is working for you, so interview them, price check and see what is posted about them on line.

You can make it a little easier on the future of your legacy if you include a note (and some money) for them to do the following to avoid identity theft:

1.Order 10 copies of the death certificate.

2.Send a copy to all three of the credit bureaus (Experian, TransUnion, Equifax) the bank, brokerage firms and insurance companies.

3.Make sure all accounts are notified, request a credit report to identify all accounts. Make sure to place a "deceased alert" on the file to stop potential scams. Remember that unless you have no money, no estate, no legal partners you may be inheriting or leaving a mess. But just in case you do receive a phone call from a "debt collector" don't say anything. Search for "credit card debt after a person dies" and look up the recent legislation on the issue (Fair Debt Collection Practices Act).

4.In addition, cancel the drivers license as well as any professional licenses.

5. Should you really care about the person and are writing an obituary, be discreet. Thieves (and debt collectors) check obits for useful details-birthdate, cities lived in etc.

For more info contact idtheftcenter.org

"FUN" THINGS TO CONSIDER

1.Traditional Burial

This is a viable alternative. I myself enjoy the quiet and solitude of a Cemetery and the thought of taking up land which developers want so very much to condo-ize fills me with joy. That being said a traditional burial is expensive. There are many aspects and each one involves a decision... and money. Which cemetery? What city? Close to relatives? In the area of your birthplace? Family plot? Religious or not? A tricked out casket or pine box (discounted at Costco)? Viewing? Service at chapel, grave site or both? This is complicated.

If you want this traditional burial, I suggest you get on it. Now. You must first buy a plot and depending on your decisions above (re: location) this may be more difficult than you think.

2.Give your body to science.

This is good on two important levels: it helps further science and medicine and you will not incur any out of pocket costs. However, there are some drawbacks. A close reading of each organizations information will outline their requirements and limitations. Science! More science!

3.Green Burial

Many of us are concerned about the environment and the burial industry is no exception. There is a website dedicated to, much like Sister Mary Ignatius, explaining it all. There you can learn the ins and outs of a green or environmentally friendly burial and find the local resources. greenburialcouncil.org

4.Cremation.

Cremation is handled by a funeral home. The Trident Society and the Neptune Society are considered funeral homes. Yes, there is a web site that gives you some helpful information on the over-all process: cremation.com. They probably are an industry sponsored site designed to look like a helpful place, but that is in fact what they do, help. A search will bring up many local and family owned business that may be less expensive, however you should make sure they will they pick up the body where you are located and arrange for the death certificate.

And if you choose cremation, you can by-pass the pesky decision of which urn to purchase (shape of a soccer ball, American flag motif, Star Trek inspired etc.) by considering the following alternatives:

If you want to continue on the "merry-go-round", you can have yourself pressed into a vinyl record (for those of you who know what that is): andvinyly.co

Remember the phrase "A diamond is forever"? In this case it is actually true (unlike marriage!) lifegem.com

If you want to branch out and imagine a life after death, come back as a tree! eternitrees.com   or thespiritree.com

And finally, for those of you who used to get seasick, consider the classic burial at sea–you won't need a patch anymore. eternalreefs.com

Now you've read my second to last chapter, I do hope you'll take the time to enact the suggestions I've made. If not for me, do it for those you love. To quote my prescient mother who peacefully resides in prime San Francisco Bay Area real estate (she got in the market early) "Clean up after yourself. Please!"

And In Conclusion

This is the point where someone else might lay out their wisdom. It would be the part where the author would include a personal insight, something touching. But as you have probably gathered, that would not be my way. This then, is my almost final words:

Ultimately there will be an end date. As much as we humans like to deny the inevitable, it is called that for a reason. Hopefully both of you will be at peace with your participation. Whilst I joke frequently and darkly, when Dad makes the move from this corporeal existence, I know I will have made the last part of his life on this planet as comfortable and hopefully as fun as possible. And as reluctant as I am to admit it, it's been fun for me too.

Isn't that the best we can ask for in life?

This Really is the Last Chapter

I know, I know. I kvetched and joked about how O.G. was the Energizer Bunny who just kept going and going…

After 13 years of living in that lovely Sherman Oaks condo, time began to take its toll on both of us. I was in the midst of my full body joint replacement campaign, something that happens when you live a full life and are bad to the bone. I was aging in direct proportion to Dad—we were simultaneously breaking down together.

Despite my stubborn "I can do it" attitude, I knew I couldn't continue on. As O.G. was declining and more dependent on personal care help, I couldn't manage that physically or emotionally. I knew something had to change or my next stop would be the San Bernardino women's prison.

So the search began for Dad's next abode began—and this part of the "caretaking trip" is NOT FUN. I found a senior living advisor to recommend housing options and brought several friends to accompany me in the search.

I discovered many options with a variety of price points. At the top of my list was the Jewish Home for the Aging. They had it all—and a luxury price tag to go with it!

- Adult Day Care
- Geriatric Clinic
- Home Care
- Transitional Care
- Short-Term Rehab
- Palliative Care

- Hospice Care
- Luxury Apartments
- Residential Care
- Dementia Care
- Psychiatric Care
- Skilled Nursing

I attempted to fill out the mere 22-page! application that asks for EVERYTHING financial. But when I was told it would cost 8K a month, I withdrew the application. I love my O.G., but not that much– we weren't rollin' like that.

The smaller care facilities, especially the "memory care" or locked units were less expensive but still out of my reach. Fortunately Dad was not a "wandering Jew" so he didn't need that level of security. At that time, Dad was still going to ONEgeneration adult daycare, so many of the services at those facilities were being provided by his wonderful daycare.

Then I looked into the next level of eldercare–a level that is not available in all states called Board and Care. So just what is a "board and care" home you ask?

A board and care home is a licensed 24-hour care property. Often operating in someone's personal home, these senior living facilities offer room, board, 24-hour staffing, assistance with bathing, dressing, medications and personal care. I discovered that many houses in the valley have been remodeled for this board and care purpose. There are usually 6 rooms for residents with their own full bathrooms. Home cooked meals are prepared for the residents, addressing individual dietary needs. The atmosphere is relaxed with a giant TV in the living room allowing residents to sit in their easy chairs and be part of the goings-on. Often the staff lives there too.

I looked at several homes and made the final decision based on the following factors: a familiar, close location; reasonably priced (no hidden fees); and it had to have a good vibe. I realize that good vibes can't be measured, but like so much of what we do in life–choosing a school, house, or partner–it's based on how we feel, going with the gut.

And my gut was right about this place. After a month of visiting my Dad and him asking me if he was going to go home, he eventually ended our visits with "Nice to see you and thanks for coming over!" I attribute this to the warm vibes from Linda (the owner) and the caregivers Sonny (cook/medicine scheduler) and JoJo (main caregiver). This amazing crew created a safe and comfortable environment for O.G. and myself–especially JoJo, who will remain my friend forever. A word of advice for those of you hiring caregivers–give them monthly tips! It seems like most of the caregivers in California– and the world–are from the Philippines. They're hardworking, compassionate folks who are frequently separated from their families and send much of their income back home. So cash is king! They are, after all, wiping your loved one's derrieres.

Most people have characterized my Dad as a nice guy. And he was– up until the end. I like to think he remembered a conversation we had

many years ago. I suggested that when it was "his time," he'd go in his sleep—easy for him and easy for me. And, damn, if that's not just what he did! The day before Dad passed, I'd taken his 2020 California Primary absentee vote by mail ballot for him to "fill" out and sign—and we even memorialized it with a photo. I won't say who he voted for, but let's just say it was a woman ☺

The next morning after I saw him, I was awakened by a call from Linda (the owner of the facility)—you know it's never good news at 7am. She said Dad had passed in the night. Finally the Energizer Bunny ran out of juice. He was just two months shy of his 98th birthday. Damn if he didn't give me the gift of an easy death. He also passed before the COVID-19 2020 lockdown. I was spared the fear and separation from my father, unlike far too many people during the pandemic. Another gift.

When I put together a slideshow for my Dad's memorial/"Shiva-lite", I discovered a few things that I had never read. I found a letter that Dad had written to his Mother dated September 16, 1945 (after the war ended on September 2, 1945). Finding little snapshots into my Dad made me realize how we never really know another person. We may think we know our parents because they retold their stories over and over, but it's only the curated bits they wanted us to see. Most of us are lazy and accept the surface without ever scratching beneath.

If there's one thing that I come away with from this chapter of my life, it's to listen more closely to the ones I love. To ask questions, even the difficult ones, because once those loved ones are gone the answers will be also. Now I realize I have the responsibility to tell my stories, to love deeply and to listen.

To borrow from the parting words of my daily meditation app, "Thank you for reading, and have a good day."